To Florence, and Al, and Daniel —C. C.

To Cathy, Rosie, Rowan, Eve, and Isaac —S. K.

A GIGANTIC thanks to Mimi Koehl from the University of California, Berkeley; Conrad Labandeira of the Smithsonian, Dr. Ed Jarzembowski of Maidstone Museum and Art Gallery, and Robert Sloan of the University of Minnesota, without whose research, knowledge, expertise, and advice this book wouldn't exist. To the Minneapolis Public Library, for their collection and the time to work on this book. To Anna and Katie Woodling, Alison and Julia Silvis, and Ted and Max Salzman for their comments on the manuscript. And to Megan McDonald, Sarah Thomson, and my family and friends, for their help and support.

SIMON & SCHUSTER BOOKS FOR YOUNG READERS

An imprint of Simon & Schuster Children's Publishing Division

1230 Avenue of the Americas, New York, New York 10020

Text copyright © 2002 by Cathy Camper

Illustrations copyright © 2002 by Steve Kirk

SIMON & SCHUSTER BOOKS FOR YOUNG READERS is a trademark of Simon & Schuster.

Book design by Heather Wood and Mark Siegel

The text for this book is set in Rotis Sans Serif.

The illustrations are rendered in watercolor.

Printed in Hong Kong

10 9 8 7 6 5 4 3 2 1

Library of Congress Cataloging-in-Publication Data

Camper, Cathy.

Bugs Before Time : prehistoric insects and their relatives / by Cathy Camper ; illustrated by Steve Kirk. — 1st ed.

p. cm.

Summary: Describes the physical characteristics, habits, and natural environment of various prehistoric insects some of which, including cockroaches, centipedes, and dragonflies, have survived into the present day.

ISBN 0-689-82092-5

1. Insects, Fossil—Juvenile literature. [1. Insects, Fossil.] I. Kirk, Steve, ill. II. Title.

QE831.C35 1999

565.7—dc21   98-22872

BUGS BEFORE TIME

Prehistoric Insects and Their Relatives

by Cathy Camper

illustrated by Steve Kirk

Simon & Schuster Books for Young Readers

New York   Lo   gapore

BUGS RULE THE EARTH

Science fiction stories and movies predict that insects will take over the world someday. But scientists who work with insects know that bugs have already taken over! There are more species of insects on earth than there are of any other living thing—nearly one million different kinds of insects that we know about, and millions more that we haven't discovered. For every pound of people on earth, there are three hundred pounds of insects.

Where did all these insects come from? Hundreds of millions of years ago, even before the days of the dinosaurs, insects and their relatives were already living and evolving. In a lot of ways, these creatures were very similar to some of the bugs you see today. But some of them were unusual even for their time—they were giants.

During prehistoric times, like today, most insects and their relatives were pretty small. But not all of them. Some ancient relatives of scorpions wouldn't fit in your bathtub. And a prehistoric dragonfly could have wings that were almost a yard across.

Why did they grow so big? Scientists think creatures like sea scorpions grew larger because they lived in the water which supported their greater weight. Other scientists think it's possible that dragonflies grew bigger during the Carboniferous period because the air may have had more oxygen in it. More oxygen would make it simpler for prehistoric insects to breathe, which meant they could grow larger. It would also create a thicker atmosphere, which could make it easier for big insects to fly.

Just as dinosaurs could be either gigantic or tiny, prehistoric insects and their relatives came in all sizes. The prehistoric dragonfly was the largest insect that ever lived, while an ancient relative of the tarantula was smaller than a pea. Today's insects are here because long, long ago creatures like these figured out ways to adapt and survive.

Friends and Relations

Insects are part of a larger group of animals called arthropods. Arthropods are animals with segmented bodies, jointed legs, and hard, armorlike shells on the outsides of their bodies. These types of shells are called exoskeletons. Since arthropods have no bones inside their bodies, they need their exoskeletons for support and protection.

Other arthropods besides insects include spiders and scorpions, horseshoe crabs, crustaceans like lobsters and crabs, and centipedes and millipedes. All of these creatures are relatives of insects.

Is It an Insect?

If you see a creepy crawly creature, how do you know it's an insect? Insects have three body parts: a head in front, a thorax in the middle, and an abdomen in back. Some insects have wings. But they all have six legs. If an unknown creature has six legs, that's a dead giveaway that it's an insect.

COCKROACHES: PREHISTORIC PESTS

They eat garbage and human hair. If you think they're everywhere, you're right. A pair of them can have 100,000 babies a year! And they've been around for 325 million years.

Long before there were humans, there were cockroaches. And over millions of years cockroaches have evolved to survive. Some modern roaches can fly and some can flatten themselves as thin as a dime to squeeze into tiny hiding places. They can run fifty steps per second. If you could do that, you could run two hundred miles an hour! A cockroach even has nerves in its head *and* its tail that act as brains. If you cut off a cockroach's head, it can still live for a couple of weeks (using the "brain" in its tail) until it finally starves to death!

Fossils of at least six hundred different species of cockroaches have been discovered. These ancient cockroaches were a lot like today's roaches—and like today's roaches, they came in all sizes. One kind could grow half a foot long. Imagine trying to stomp on a cockroach almost as big as your shoe!

Cockroach Cuisine

Modern cockroaches will munch on anything from spilled food, to shoe polish, to human eyebrows and fingernails. One roach can live for a month on the glue of a postage stamp. Prehistoric roaches ate mostly rotting plants, and maybe decaying animal tissue.

Cockroaches shed their hardened skin, or exoskeleton, several times during their lives. If a modern cockroach loses a leg or antennae, it gets a new one with its new skin.

Ancient Roommates

When distant human ancestors first took shelter in caves about three million years ago, cockroaches discovered that their food and garbage were great sources of food. Roaches have been living with people ever since.

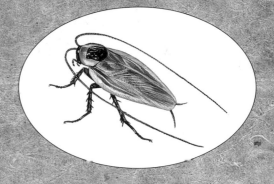

The cerci are two sensitive prongs on the cockroach's rear end that alert the insect to possible danger and help it to escape quickly.

The front pair of wings protected the roach's more delicate back wings, so it could crawl into tiny spaces.

Female prehistoric roaches had a long tube-shaped organ called an ovipositor, which they used to lay eggs in the soil. Modern cock-roaches have a shorter ovipositor, or one that is inside their bodies, and lay their eggs in a leathery egg case called an ootheca.

ANCIENT REMAINS: HOW FOSSILS ARE FORMED

No human beings existed back when giant dragonflies flew through the air or ancient cockroaches crawled in the mud. So how do scientists know what prehistoric bugs looked like?

Most of what scientists know about prehistoric bugs comes from fossils. A fossil is what's left of an ancient plant or animal that has been preserved for millions of years. From fossils and other clues, like insects preserved in amber, scientists can figure out a prehistoric insect's size and shape—how big its wings were, how many eyes and legs it had. (But they usually can't tell what color it was, so when artists paint prehistoric insects, they have to guess about the color.)

Not too many prehistoric insects lasted long enough to become fossils. Many dead insects were squashed, destroyed by rain or wind, or gobbled up by hungry animals before they could be fossilized. When they don't have good fossils, scientists try to guess what prehistoric insects looked like by comparing them with their descendants—living insects.

FROZEN IN GOLD

Amber is the ancient resin, or sap, of plants like conifers or *Hymenaea*, a relative of modern peas and beans.

- When plant bark splits open, gluey sap oozes out.
- An insect is stuck and covered in the resin, where its body is preserved.
- Light and air turn the sap hard.
- The sap is buried and later covered by sea water.
- Over millions of years, chemical changes take place that turn the resin into hard, clear amber.

FOSSIL FUEL

Coal is made of the fossilized bodies of plants, insects, and other animals from the Carboniferous period, when huge swamps covered most of the earth.

- When prehistoric insects died, they sank into the swamp mud or peat.

- The insects' bodies were buried by fallen leaves and dead plants.
- If they didn't decay first, the dead plants and insects were pressed tightly together for many years.
- Time, temperature, and pressure turned these plants and insect bodies first into peat and then into coal.

TURNING TO STONE

Some of our best clues about how prehistoric insects looked come from stone fossils.

- The insect dies.
- Its body rots, so that only its hard outer shell, or exoskeleton, remains.
- The exoskeleton is covered with dirt or mud.
- Over the years, pressure hardens the dirt and mud into rocks.
- Sometimes the actual hard substance of the insect's exoskeleton, called chitin, is preserved. Other times, the exoskeleton may decay and be replaced by minerals, which are in the water flowing through the rock. The minerals become a fossil: a stone copy, or mold, of the insect, showing its exact size and shape.
- Fossils may lie hidden underground for many years, until the rock wears away or is forced up to the surface.

LEAVING THEIR MARK

Insects can leave footprints, wing prints, bite marks, and skin texture prints for us to study.

- An insect's body is pressed into wet mud, sand, or clay, leaving an imprint.
- Over millions of years the dirt hardens into rock, preserving the imprint forever.

EURYPTERIDS: ARMORED MONSTERS OF THE PRIMORDIAL SEAS

The quiet coastal lagoons of four hundred million years ago may have seemed peaceful and safe. But below the water's surface lurked danger. This is where eurypterids lived—giant sea scorpions, some of the fiercest predators of the ocean.

A eurypterid was like a swimming fort. It was covered in armor and had two jointed pincers which it used for attacking prey. On the end of their tails, some eurypterids had a tail spike, or telson, that could deliver a nasty sting to whatever they caught with their claws. And to help it move quickly through the water, a eurypterid had two paddle-shaped legs.

At first eurypterids only lived in the ocean, but eventually they moved to salty swamps, and perhaps, rivers and streams. Today's smaller scorpions may share a common ancestor with these fierce swimming hunters.

The back four pairs of legs were often used for walking. Sometimes these walking legs were short, located near the mouth, and used to hold food. Sometimes they had teeth on them!

Bigger Than a Bread Box

Most eurypterids were five to seven inches long, but there were some that grew up to seven feet—as long as a couch. Some may have been up to fifteen feet! As they grew bigger, eurypterids molted their exoskeletons, and they may have added more segments as they grew longer.

Backstroke

Eurypterids swam upside down. They used their rear paddle-shaped limbs and fanned the plates on their stomachs to move through the water.

Eurypterids had between five to six pairs of appendages. The front pair, called *chelicerae*, were used as mouthparts. They had pincers on them, for catching prey. Sometimes they had spikes on them too.

Depending on its shape, the telson was used as a stinger, a paddle, or a lever for digging.

Eurypterids are arthropods, but not insects. Like horseshoe crabs, spiders, and scorpions, arthropods have two main body parts (a head and an abdomen) instead of three, like an insect.

TRILOBITES: SUPERSUCKERS

Imagine an armored **underwater vacuum cleaner** that runs on its own power. That's kind of what a trilobite looked like as it inched along the ocean floor sucking food into its mouth. Trilobites' mouths were located underneath their bodies, and most of them **siphoned up food from the mud and sand** as they moved along the bottom of the ocean. Some drifted freely in the water.

Trilobites were very successful animals. There were ten thousand different species, and they survived for three hundred million years before they became extinct. Most trilobites were only two or three inches long, but some were over two feet—**as long as a grown-up's arm!**—and may have weighed about ten pounds.

Trilobites are the first known creatures with compound eyes. Their eyes were made up of many lenses, which means they saw many images at once. As they evolved, some trilobites' eyes shrank until they disappeared, others grew larger, and some were on platforms or stalks.

▼

A Charmed Life

Trilobites have fascinated people for a long time. Human remains found in France from fifteen thousand years ago include a fossil trilobite with a hole in it, to be worn as a necklace. Long ago, when the Ute Indians of the western United States found trilobite fossils, they collected them as charms and gave them the name "timpe khanitza pachavee," which means "little bug like stone house in."

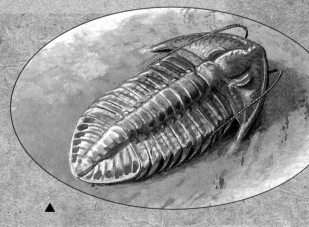

▲

A trilobite might have planted its genal spines in the ocean floor so it could sit facing into the water's current, which would bring food within its reach and carry away waste material.

Plated for Protection

A trilobite's outer armor was jointed, like a sow bug or armadillo, and some trilobites could roll up into a ball to defend themselves. When a trilobite got too big for its exoskeleton, it would stick the genal spine of its head into the mud, and crawl forward out of the opening, or suture, between its head and body.

◄ The front pair of appendages, near the mouth, were like sensing antennae. Other appendages were used for walking and had feathery gills for breathing and swimming. They also had an organ for chewing and digesting food.

▲

A trilobite's thorax is divided into three sections, or lobes (trilobite means "three lobes"). Trilobites aren't insects; they have only a head and thorax, and they have more legs than insects do.

INSECT EVOLUTION—
WHERE DID THEY COME FROM?

Which came first, cockroaches or butterflies? Actually, **the oldest insect fossils** are of bugs called bristletails, and are from 390 million years ago. But that's only the oldest insect *fossil*. Insects were undoubtedly around for millions of years before bristletails. What did these earlier insects look like? **No one knows.** No fossils of them have ever been found. But we do know that they probably evolved from crustaceans **like today's lobsters and crabs**, or from creatures like centipedes and millipedes.

By looking at insects, we can tell which came first and which evolved later. Their bodies give us clues.

For a long time scientists believed flowering plants and insects evolved together. Insects developed mouthparts to help them get nectar, and flowering plants evolved to attract insects with their scents, nectar, and bright colors. Recently scientists discovered the theory was wrong. When they looked at fossils, they found insects had developed mouthparts to eat plants long before plants had flowers.

The most advanced insects, like beetles, have wings that can fold up or be hidden under wing covers to protect them.

More advanced insects, like dragonflies, have wings that can't fold up; they lie out to the side when the insect is at rest.

The earliest insects, like silverfish, have no wings.

Why Change?

Why do insects change their shape halfway through life? Because it has helped them survive. Since the larva, or early stage, and the adult insect can evolve separately, an insect can change quickly to fit into its environment. While a caterpillar evolved different mouthparts to munch on leaves, the adult butterfly developed different mouthparts to feed on nectar. By adapting so rapidly, insects can adapt to compete with other creatures for living space or to live in places where nothing else can survive.

More advanced insects, like grasshoppers, go through incomplete metamorphosis. They have one basic shape when they're young, and molt several times as they grow larger. But after the final molt, they have a full set of wings and are able to reproduce.

Advanced insects, like butterflies, wasps, bees, and ants, go through complete metamorphosis. They start life as caterpillars or larvae, then molt into a resting stage, or pupa. When they finally emerge as adult insects, they don't look anything like the first two stages.

Early insects, like bristletails, look the same their whole lives. They shed, or molt, their exoskeleton as they grow larger but never change shape.

CENTIPEDES AND MILLIPEDES: A FOOT OF FEET

One hundred legs. Two—three—*four* hundred legs. Moving in waves. All attached to **one long wiggling creature**. That's what centipedes and millipedes look like today. Their ancestors from hundreds of millions of years ago probably looked much the same—but they may have lived in water instead of on dry land.

The largest centipedes alive today are about ten inches long; the largest living millipedes are about a foot long. Some people keep these **big millipedes as pets**! But you wouldn't want to have kept some prehistoric multi-leggers in your house. Some ancient centipedes were over three feet long, and one kind of prehistoric millipede, called "Arthropleura," could be twice that long—six feet. That's **probably bigger than your mom**!

Don't Tread on Me!

In their first set of legs (which acted as fangs) prehistoric centipedes had poison glands, just like modern ones do today. They used their bites to paralyze prey, or to fight off attacking creatures.

This millipede, called "Acantherpestes," probably used the spines that grew out of its sides to keep predators away.

A Lot of Legs

Centipedes and millipedes were named for their many legs. Centipede means "hundreds of legs"; millipede means "thousands of legs." Today, baby millipedes start out with only three pairs of legs, and baby centipedes with seven; but each time they molt they acquire more legs.

Just like modern ones, prehistoric millipedes had two pairs of legs on each of their body segments (up to two hundred pairs), while centipedes had only one pair per segment (up to 170 pairs).

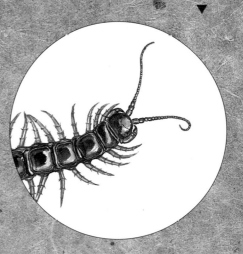

Millipedes and centipedes have way too many body parts and legs to be insects. Millipedes are in the class of creatures called "Diploda," while centipedes belong to the class called "Chilopoda."

A giant spiderlike creature called "Megarachne," lived three hundred million years ago. Its abdomen was thirteen inches long and its leg span was about twenty inches. It could have reached two-thirds of the way around a basketball!

DRAGONFLIES: RULERS OF THE SKY

It's three hundred million years ago. The world is swampy, the air is hot and humid. There are no people or dinosaurs. A few large amphibians doze in the warm mud. Horsetails, mosses, and ferns as big as trees bake in the still air.

Suddenly, there's a loud whirring sound. What is it? Birds, bats, pterosaurs, and planes don't exist in this ancient world.

Flying overhead is the biggest insect that ever lived! Protodonata were prehistoric dragonflies that ruled the skies during the Carboniferous period. In many ways these prehistoric dragonflies were just like the dragonflies you see today. But their wings reached thirty inches from tip to tip! If they flew through an average door-way, their wing tips might just brush either side.

What's for Dinner?

Today's dragonflies can catch flies and mosquitoes in midair. What did prehistoric dragonflies eat? Probably cockroaches, mayflies, and maybe even small amphibians.

The dragonfly used its barbed legs to catch insects in flight. The legs and mouthparts surrounded the prey like a cage.

▼

Some modern dragonflies have eyes with over 20,000 lenses, and use 80 percent of their brains for vision. Like their descendants, ancient dragonflies could probably see in twilight and detect even the slightest motion nearby.

Open Wide

Dragonflies got their names from their big mouths! The scientific name for modern dragonflies is "Odonata," which comes from the Greek word meaning "tooth." Dragonflies have big mouthparts and jaws. Prehistoric dragonflies are called "Protodonata." "Proto" means "before," so "Protodonata" means "before Odonata."

The front and back pair of wings on prehistoric (and modern) dragonflies moved separately from each other. Dragonflies could move up, down, and sideways just like a helicopter.

Young dragonflies (called naiads) looked nothing like their parents. The naiads had a mouthpart like a lower lip with a claw on it, called a labial mask. They used this claw to grab their prey and haul it to their mouths. Protodanatan naiads lived in water, and they could have been as big as a frog or salamander.

WING THING: NEW IDEAS ABOUT FLIGHT

The fossils of the earliest insects have no wings, but later insects like dragonflies became **great flyers.** How did insects get wings? The **skeletons** of flying animals like birds, bats, and pterosaurs, show that they originally had four legs, and then their front limbs evolved into wings. But **insects are different.** They have **six legs—** *and* **wings.**

Where did insects' wings come from? Scientists have a lot of ideas.

Wings That Sing

Although wings are used mainly to fly, some insects use them for a completely different purpose—to make noise! Arthropods were probably the first animals to communicate through sound. Most creatures make sound using their vocal chords and their breath, to express emotion. But insects can use their exoskeletons to make all kinds of noises—strumming, beating, vibrating, clicking, and blowing out air. Even when you can't see them, the sounds insects make let you know they are there.

Theory #1

Insects developed lobes, or smooth flat growths, out of the sides of their bodies. These lobes worked like solar panels to heat up the insect with the warmth of sunlight, or possibly as decorations to attract a mate. As the lobes grew larger, insects were able to use them to parachute or glide, and eventually to fly.

Testing...

Two scientists built models of prehistoric insects and tried to heat them up and fly them in a wind tunnel. Wing lobes under a centimeter didn't help the insect fly, but they did help keep it warm. Wing lobes over a centimeter long helped the insect glide. And the bigger the insect, the smaller the wing lobes needed to keep it in the air. This could mean that insects first developed wing lobes to keep them warm, but as the lobes *and* the bugs got bigger, the lobes helped them fly.

Theory #2

Ancient water insects could have used their gills like fins to move through the water. The gills eventually turned into wing lobes that let the insect skim over the top of water, rather than swim below the surface—a quicker way to move. The wing lobes grew bigger and bigger until insects could actually use them to fly.

Testing...

Mayflies and stoneflies are some of the most primitive insects alive today, and they use their wings to skim over the surface of the water. A scientist and his assistant trimmed the wings of stoneflies to various sizes. Even short wings, though they couldn't be used for flight, helped the insect skim over the water—and the bigger the wings, the faster it could move. This could mean that early insects first began to skim instead of swim—and later they learned to fly.

Which theory is correct? Nobody knows for sure.
Scientists will look at the fossils to see what really happened.

ANTS AND WASPS: COLONIES OF CRAWLING CREATURES.

To a prehistoric mammal, an anthill or wasp nest might look like a lunch box **full of tender yummy insects** to eat. But it would learn quickly that **this lunch bites—and stings!** Ants and wasps are social insects, which means they spend their lives together. The queen lays eggs; female workers find food, build the nest, and raise the young; males mate with the queen.

Ants and wasps live in colonies today because, millions of years ago, some prehistoric wasps evolved to live together. Scientists think that prehistoric female wasps first built their nests in the ground and **hunted down** insects to feed their young. The mother wasp and her daughters continued to live together, but the daughters no longer laid eggs themselves. Instead, **they helped their mother** raise more young sisters. Gradually, these ancient wasps evolved into the first wasp and ant colonies.

Among prehistoric wasps, only the females could sting, just like wasps today. Wasps sting to protect themselves or to kill prey.

▼

The Missing Link

For a long time, scientists had no proof that ants and wasps were related. Then a piece of amber ninety million years old was found with two fossilized insects in it, the "missing links" between wasps and ants. These insects had short mandibles (or jaws) with only two teeth, like wasps. They also had pinched waists, no wings, and a gland on their thorax like modern ants.

Gigantic Ants

The largest known ants living or extinct lived about 42 million years ago. Only the remains of queens and male ants have been found. Their bodies were over one inch long, and the front wings of the queens were one to two and a half inches long.

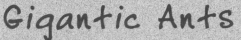

An ant's sting carries poison that comes from a gland near the stinger. Most ants bite, and some can sting or spray an acid on their prey's wounds to paralyze it.

Ants have a node (a bumplike growth) on their waist that makes them different from wasps. Wasps have a pinched-in "wasp waist," called the "metasoma," at the part of the abdomen that connects to the thorax.

SPIDERS: WEB-WEAVERS OF THE WORLD

As a tiny prehistoric ant hurries back to the ant colony, it stumbles on an invisible thread. The more it struggles to free itself, the sooner it will die. Every move tells a prehistoric spider that its next meal is waiting!

A spider's ability to spin thread evolved over millions of years. Prehistoric spiders probably had glands at the base of their legs that left trails of body waste behind them. These trails helped spiders find their way back home or lead them to mates. As spiders evolved, different body parts began to get rid of wastes. But the glands changed into spinnerets, and the trails they now left were made of longer-lasting silk. Early spiders spun silk "pockets," to line their holes, and triplines of silk around their homes. If something touched these triplines, the motion would alert the spider. These simple threads evolved into the first sheetlike webs.

Spiders are arachnids, not insects. Arachnids have eight legs instead of six, no wings or antennae, and two body parts instead of three.

Meaty Milkshakes

Prehistoric spiders didn't eat their food—they drank it! With their fangs, they injected poison into prey to make it hold still. The spiders tied their victims up with silk and injected them with a substance that made their bodies dissolve. Then they sucked their meal down, just like a milkshake! Today, this is how a large spider like a tarantula can eat an animal like a frog.

Hairy and Scary

Scientists have found fossils of mygalomorphs, or "bird-eating" spiders, that are 240 million years old. Mygalomorphs alive today include the tarantula, which can have a leg span of up to ten inches. These prehistoric spiders were much smaller, with bodies that were only about a quarter inch long.

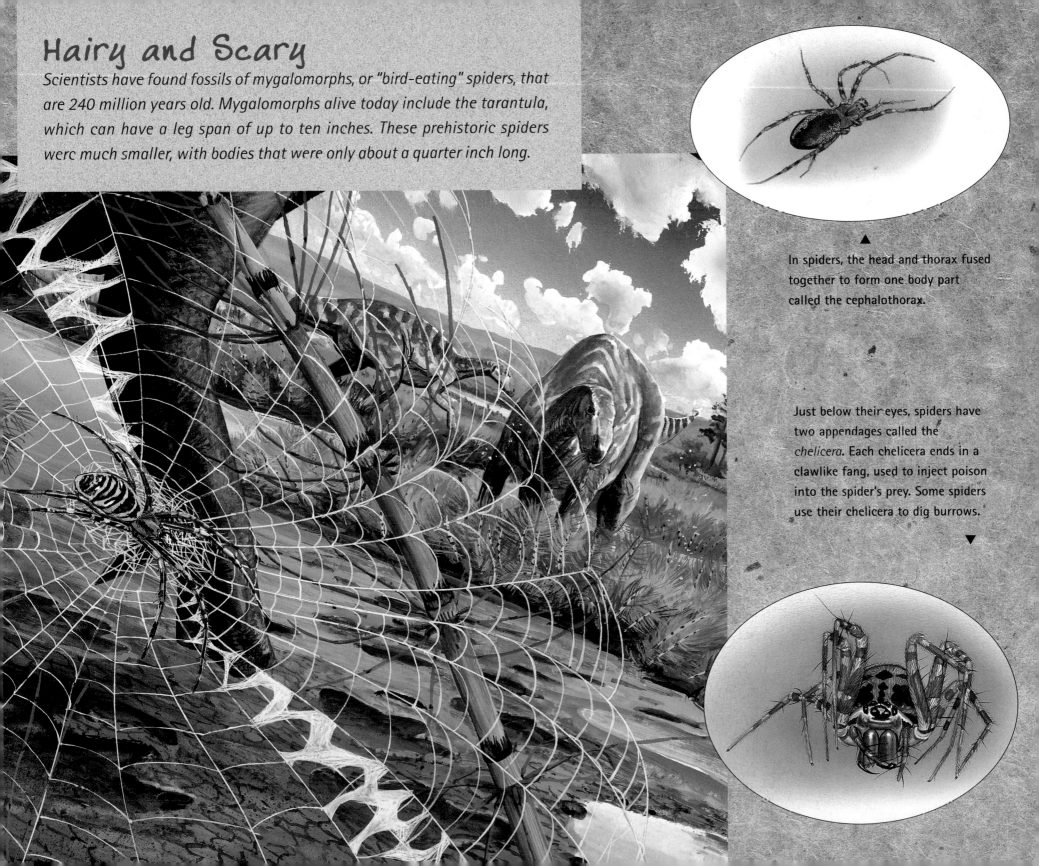

▲

In spiders, the head and thorax fused together to form one body part called the cephalothorax.

Just below their eyes, spiders have two appendages called the *chelicera*. Each chelicera ends in a clawlike fang, used to inject poison into the spider's prey. Some spiders use their chelicera to dig burrows.

▼

BEETLES, BUTTERFLIES, BUGS GALORE!

Some of the insects that are familiar to us have been around for a long time, while others evolved fairly recently. Moths, for example, have been around for two hundred million years, while bees evolved only 85 million years ago. Some prehistoric insects, like beetles, would be easy to recognize, while others, like Titanopterous, would look like monster insects if they were still around today!

Beetle Mania

Today there are **more species of beetles** in the world than any other kind of insect. Beetles have been around for 270 million years, and they have found many ways to survive. A hard shell that protects their wings lets them **crawl** and **burrow**, as well as **fly**, so they can live in many places. The earliest prehistoric beetles probably ate wood, but their descendants can **eat almost anything**—plants, animals, and other insects, living or dead. Beetle fossils from about one million years ago are the same species as the beetles we see today.

Flying Colors

Some of the **prettiest insects** around today were some of the more recent to evolve. Scientists think butterflies evolved from moths, and that moths and an insect called a caddis fly both evolved from a common ancestor. The earliest fossils of butterflies go back around sixty million years. They probably ate plants in the **pea and cabbage** families, which had also evolved around that time. Most ancient butterflies had wingspans of around two inches, and looked a lot like modern butterflies.

Chirp and Hop

Just as cats chase grasshoppers today, small insect-eating dinosaurs may have tried to catch grasshoppers and their relatives in prehistoric times. The group of insects called "Orthoptera" (which means "straight wings") has been around at least 325 million years. Fossils from around 305 million years ago show these insects had already evolved the big hind legs they used for jumping. As they evolved, they developed the ability to make noise by rubbing their wings together, and they developed organs to hear the sounds they made. Modern Orthopterans include grasshoppers, crickets, locusts, and katydids.

A Singing Giant

Titanopterous was a grasshopper-like insect that lived from about 226 to 208 million years ago. It had a wingspan of about fourteen inches—a little more than a foot. Like crickets, it had sound-producing files on its wings. And although it didn't have big jumping legs like a grasshopper, it did have spines on its front legs, which makes some scientists think it was a predator.

EPILOGUE

Why do scientists study insects? There are good reasons to study living insects. We need to learn how to control them, so they don't eat crops, cause illness in people and animals, and become a general nuisance. And we can also learn from them how to get products like silk (from silkworms) and honey (from bees). Today, scientists have found that information is one of the best "products" to come from insects. One scientist observed how insects like cockroaches and centipedes walk by filming their progress over a brightly lit gelatin floor. From what he's learned, he hopes to build robots with legs like a bug's that could one day walk on Mars.

But why study insects from millions of years ago? Scientists can learn more about modern insects by studying their ancestors. And insects have also been around for a very long time. Their adaptations and changes over hundreds of millions of years can teach us a lot about how life on this planet survives, and their remains can help solve puzzles about how life evolved and how all living things are related.

Insects could be called the most successful life form on earth—the most numerous, varied, adaptable, and best fitted to survive. Plus, much of the natural world depends on insects. If all insects were to die out, many plants and animals would die too. But if all humans became extinct, the natural world would still do just fine. By studying insects, maybe people can learn to coexist as well as insects do with the natural world.

ROCK AND ROLL

Insects have changed over the **four hundred million years** of the earth's history but so has the earth itself. In trying to find out what prehistoric life was like, scientists have to look not just at plants and animals but also at the **location of the continents where they lived** and the changes in weather.

All of the earth's continents are attached to plates which move about an inch a year on the ocean of **molten rock deep under the surface** of the planet. Over millions of years, the continents have changed shape and position.

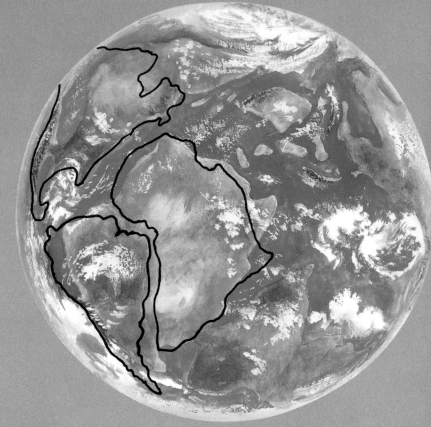

During the **Triassic period**, 220 million years ago, the continents were joined in one land mass called Pangaea. The climate was warm, with deserts and some shallow seas. Some scientists think that a drop in sea levels caused many animals to become extinct.

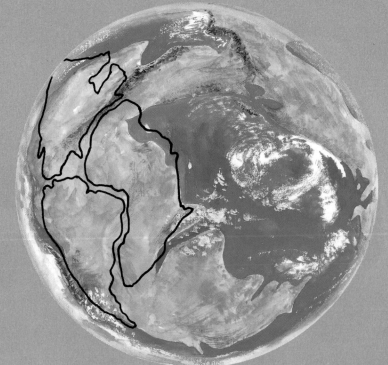

During the **Jurassic period**, two hundred million years ago, Pangaea split into two new supercontinents, Gondwanaland and Laurasia. The climate was warm and stable, with little difference between the seasons. This was the age of the dinosaurs. Even Antarctica was warm enough for dinosaurs and plants to live there.

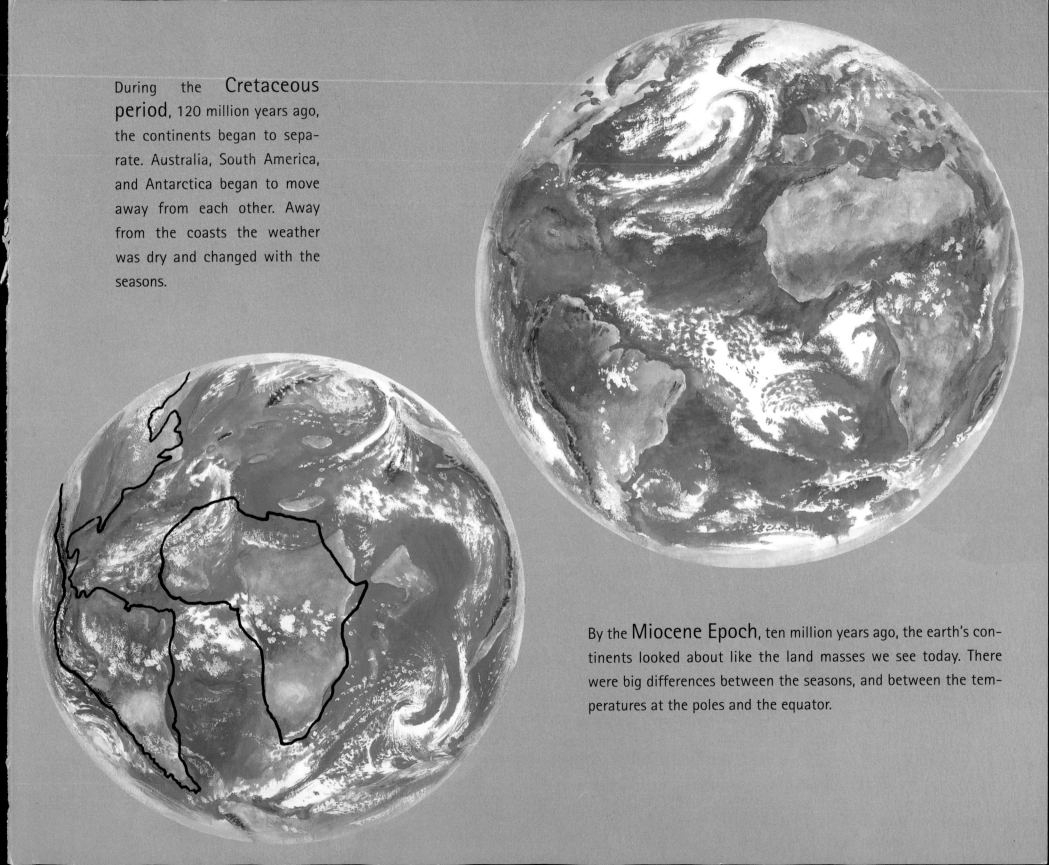

During the **Cretaceous period**, 120 million years ago, the continents began to separate. Australia, South America, and Antarctica began to move away from each other. Away from the coasts the weather was dry and changed with the seasons.

By the **Miocene Epoch**, ten million years ago, the earth's continents looked about like the land masses we see today. There were big differences between the seasons, and between the temperatures at the poles and the equator.

GEOLOGIC TIME

The earth is about 4.6 billion years old. If an average person is 76 years old, it would take 6,052,631,578 human life-times to last 4.6 billion years! To keep track of the earth's long history, scientists divide it into eras and periods.

Ancient arthropod relatives of insects lived in the ocean until about 420 million years ago. Then some of these primitive relatives of insects, spiders, centipedes, millipedes, and sea scorpions crawled onto land. Gradually they began to evolve into the many kinds of insects there are today. By the time Tyrannosaurus rex was around, most insects had already evolved to look pretty much like they do today.

PRECAMBRIAN PERIOD — 4.5 billion–570 million years ago
The earth and its atmosphere were formed. — 4,600 million years ago
The oldest animal fossils ever found were created. — 700 million years ago
The first trilobites comb the ocean floor. — 540 million years ago

CAMBRIAN PERIOD — 570–510 million years ago
Eurypterids terrorize the seas. — 540–250 million years ago

ORDOVICIAN PERIOD — 510–439 million years ago
Primitive fish evolve. — 500 million years ago

SILURIAN PERIOD — 439–409 million years ago
Arthropods move onto land. — 420 million years ago

CARBONIFEROUS PERIOD
362–322 million years ago

The earliest cockroaches crawl through the coal forests.   330 million years ago

The first flying insects swoop through the air.   330 million years ago

Prehistoric dragonflies zip through the skies.   330 million years ago

Grasshoppers and crickets hop around the ground.   325 million years ago

PERMIAN PERIOD
290–245 million years ago

The earliest dinosaurs appear.   250 million years ago

TRIASSIC PERIOD
245–208 million years ago

The land masses are joined in Pangaea.   225 million years ago

The earliest mammals develop.   210 million years ago

JURASSIC PERIOD
208–145 million years ago

Birds appear.   150 million years ago

Wasps hunt their prey.   145 million years ago

CRETACEOUS PERIOD
145–65 million years ago

The first flowers begin to bloom.   125 million years ago

Ants crawl.   110 million years ago

Bees buzz.   85 million years ago

Butterflies flutter.   60 million years ago

Tyrannosaurus rex roams the earth.   80–65 million years ago

DEVONIAN PERIOD
409–362 million years ago

The first primitive plants appear.   408 million years ago

Centipedes and millipedes develop.   400 million years ago

Spiders first appear.   400 million years ago

The first known true insect, the bristletail, appears.   390 million years ago

Fish crawl out onto land.   375 million years ago

TERTIARY PERIOD
66–5 million years ago

PLIOCENE EPOCH
5–1.6 million years ago

Prehistoric humans develop.   3–1 million years ago

HOLOCENE EPOCH
.01 million years ago–now

Modern humans walk the earth.   100,000 years ago

CHILDREN'S BOOKS

Bailey, Jill and Seddon, Tony. *Young Oxford Book of the Prehistoric World*. Oxford University Press, 1995.

Busby, Coenrads, Willis and Roots. *The Nature Company Guides to Rocks and Fossils*. 1996.

Cross, Wilbur. *Coal*. Chicago: Children's Press, 1983.

Dewan, Ted. *Inside Dinosaurs and Other Prehistoric Creatures*. New York: A Doubleday Book for Young Readers, 1993.

Dixon, Dougal. *Dougal Dixon's Dinosaurs*. Honesdale, PA: Boyds Mills Press, 1993.

Facklam, Margery. *The Big Bug Book*. Boston: Little Brown Publishing, 1994.

Farndon, John. *Dictionary of the Earth*. New York: Dorling Kindersley, 1994.

Gaffney, Michael. *Secret Forests*. Golden Books, 1994.

Goor, Ron. *Insect Metamorphosis: From Egg to Adult*. New York: Atheneum, 1990.

Hansen, Michael C. *Coal, How It Is Found and Used*. Hillsdale, NJ: Enslow Publishers, 1990.

Kaufman, John. *Flying Giants of Long Ago*. New York: Crowell, 1984.

Kerby, Mona. *Cockroaches*. New York: Franklin Watts, 1989.

Kraft, Betsy Harvey. *Coal*. New York: Franklin Watts, 1982.

Lauber, Patricia. *Dinosaurs Walked Here, and Other Stories Fossils Tell*. New York: Macmillan Publishing Company, 1992.

Lessem, Don. *Dinosaur Worlds*. Honesdale, PA: Boyds Mills Press, 1996.

Lindsay, William. *Prehistoric Life*. (Eyewitness Books). New York: Alfred A. Knopf, 1994.

Mound, Laurence. *Insect*. (Eyewitness Books). New York: Alfred A. Knopf, 1990.

Parker, Steve. *Inside Dinosaurs and Other Prehistoric Creatures*. New York: Doubleday Books for Young Readers, 1993.

Peters, David. *Giants of Land, Sea, and Air, Past and Present*. New York: Alfred A. Knopf, 1986.

Peters, David. *Strange Creatures*. New York: Morrow Junior Books, 1992.

Preston-Mafham, Ken. *Discovering Centipedes and Millipedes*. New York: Bookwright Press, 1990.

Pringle, Laurence. *Cockroaches: Here, There and Everywhere*. New York: Thomas Y. Crowell Company, 1971.

Pringle, Laurence P. *Scorpion Man: Exploring the World of Scorpions*. New York: C. Scribner's Sons, 1994.

Sattler, Helen. *Our Patchwork Planet*. New York: Lothrop, Lee and Shepard, 1995.

Visual Dictionary of Prehistoric Life. New York: Dorling Kindersley, Inc., 1995.

Walker, Cyril and David Ward. *Fossil*. (Eyewitness Handbooks). New York: Dorling Kindersley, Inc., 1992.

ADULT BOOKS

Brusca, Richard C. and Brusca, Gary J. *Invertebrates*. Sunderland, MA: Sinauer Associates, Inc., 1990.

Callahan, Philip S. *The Evolution of Insects*. New York: Holiday House, 1972.

Carter, David. *Butterflies and Moths*. New York: Dorling Kindersley, Inc., 1992.

Case, Gerard R. *A Pictorial Guide to Fossils*. New York: Van Nordstrand, 1982.

Cornwell, P. B. *The Cockroach*. London: Hutchinson, 1968.

Davies, R. G. *Outlines of Entomology*. London and New York: Chapman and Hall, 1988.

Emmel, Thomas C., Marc C. Minno, and Boyce A. Drummond. *Florissant Butterflies: A Guide to the Fossil and Present Day Species of Central Colorado*. Stanford, CA: Stanford University Press, 1992.

Encyclopedia of Prehistoric Life. Edited by Rodney Steel and Anthony Harvey. New York: McGraw Hill, 1979.

Ewing, Arthur W. *Arthropod Bioacoustics: Neurobiology and Behavior*. Ithaca, NY: Cornell University Press, 1989.

Evans, Arthur V. and Charles L. Bellamy. *An Inordinate Fondness for Beetles*. New York: Henry Holt, 1996.

Feltwell, John. *The Natural History of Butterflies*. New York: Facts on File Publishing, 1986.

Fenton, Carroll Lane and Mildred Adams Fenton. *The Fossil Book*. Garden City, NY: Doubleday, 1958.

Fossil Invertebrates. Richard S. Boardman, Senior Editor; Alan H. Cheetham, Albert J. Rowell, Editors. Palo Alto, CA: Blackwell Scientific Publications, 1987.

Gordon, David George. *The Complete Cockroach*. Berkeley, CA: Tenspeed Press, 1996.

Harland, W. B.; R. L. Armstrong, A. V. Cox, L. E. Craig, A. G. Smith and David Smith. *Geologic Time Scale*. Cambridge: Cambridge University Press, 1989.

Hillyard, Paul. *The Book of the Spider*. New York: Random House, 1994.

Hubbell, Sue. *A Book of Bees*. New York: Random House, 1988.

Hubbell, Sue. *Broadsides from the Other Orders: A Book of Bugs*. New York: Random House, 1993.

Holldobler, Bert and Edward O. Wilson. *The Ants*. Cambridge, MA, and London, England: Belknap Press of Harvard University Press, 1990.

Holldobler, Bert and Edward O. Wilson. *Journey to the Ants: A Story of Scientific Exploration*. Cambridge, MA, and London, England: Belknap Press of Harvard University Press, 1994.

Levi, Herbert W. and Lorna R. Levi. *Spiders and Their Kin*. New York: Golden Press, 1968.

Levi-Setti, Riccardo. *Trilobites*. 2nd ed. Chicago: University of Chicago Press, 1993.

Matsen, Bradford. *Planet Ocean: A Story of Life, the Sea, and Dancing to the Fossil Record*. Berkeley, CA: Ten Speed Press, 1994.

Milne, Lorus Johnson. *The Audobon Society Field Guide to North American Insects and Spiders*. New York: Alfred A. Knopf, 1980.

O'Toole, Christopher. *Alien Empire: An Exploration of the Lives of Insects*. New York: HarperCollins, 1995.

Pearse, Vicki, John Pearse, Mildred Buchsbaum, and Ralph Buchsbaum. *Living Invertebrates*. Palo Alto, CA: Blackwell Scientific Publications, and Pacific Grove, CA: Boxwood Press, 1987.

Pinna, Giovanni. *The Illustrated Encyclopedia of Fossils*. Translated by Jay Hyams. New York: Facts on File Publishing, 1990.

Poinar, George D. *The Quest for Life in Amber*. Reading, MA: Addison-Wesley, 1994.

Preston-Mafham, Rod and Ken. *Spiders of the World*. New York: Facts on File Publishing, 1984.

Russell, Dale A. *An Odyssey in Time: The Dinosaurs of North America*. Minocqua, WI: NorthWord Press in association with the National Museum of Natural Sciences, 1989.

Sharov, A. G. *Phylogeny of the Orthopteroidea*. Jerusalem, Israel: Israel Program for Scientific Translations, 1971.

Smith, A. G., David G. Smith and B. M. Funnell. *Atlas of Mesozoic and Cenozoic Coastlines*. Cambridge: Cambridge University Press, 1994.

Treatise on Invertebrate Paleontology. Roger L. Kaesler, Editor. Part R, Arthropoda 4, volumes 3 and 4, by F. M. Carpenter. Lawrence, Kansas, and Boulder, Colorado: Geological Society of America, Inc. and the University of Kansas 1992.

Waldbauer, Gilbert. *Insects Through the Seasons*. Cambridge, MA: Harvard University Press, 1996.

Whittington, H. B. *Trilobites*. Woodbridge, England: Boydell Press, 1992.

MAGAZINE ARTICLES

Anderson, Ian. "Is Australian Fossil the Ancestor of All Insects?" *New Scientist*, August 17, 1991, 15.

Anonymous. "Flight of Conjecture," *Scientific American*, April 1986, 66B.

Anonymous. "Remains of the Prey," *Discover*, June 1993, 13.

Bowler, Sue. "When Bird-eating Spiders Ruled the Earth," *New Scientist*, June 20, 1992, 18.

Duncan, I. J. and D. E. G. Briggs. "Three-dimensionally Preserved Insects," *Nature*, May 2, 1996, 30-31.

Grimaldi, David A. "Captured in Amber," *Scientific American*, April 1996, 84-91.

I.D. The International Design Magazine. "The Bug Issue." September/October 1997.

Koehl, M. A. R. and Joel G. Kingsolver. "Aerodynamics, Thermoregulation and the Evolution of Insect Wings: Differential Scaling and Evolutionary Change," *Evolution*, vol. 39, 1985, 488-504.

Lewin, Roger. "On the Origin of Insect Wings," *Science*, October 25, 1985, 428-429.

Marden, James H. "Flying Lessons From a Flightless Insect," *Natural History*, February 1995, 4, 6, 8.

Marden, James H. and Melissa G. Kramer. "Surface-skimming Stoneflies: A Possible Intermediate Stage in Insect Flight Evolution," *Science*, October 21, 1994, 427-430.

Menon, Shanti. "Insects of the Oxygeniferous," *Discover*, September 1995, 32.

Mereson, Amy and Glenn Butash. "Battling the Perfect Bug: Sophisticated Strategies for Conquering the Cockroach," *Science Digest*, October 1985.

Morell, Virginia. "Golden Window on a Lost World," *Discover*, August 1993, 44-52.

Pennisi, Elizabeth. "Did Insects Skim Before They Flew?" *Science News*, October 29, 1994, 276.

Seldon, P. A. "The Biggest Spider," *Secretary's New Letter* (British Arachnological Society), vol. 36, 1983, 4-5.

Shear, William A. "Untangling the Evolution of the Web," *American Scientist*, May-June, 1994, 256-266.

Spiessbach, Kathleen. "The Eyes of Bees," *Discover*, Sept. 1996, 32.

Wilford, John Noble. "Long before Flowering Plants, Insects Evolved Ways to Use Them," *The New York Times*, August 3, 1993, C1, C10.

Wuethrich, B. "Scientists Upset Insect Orthodoxies," *Science News*, July 17, 1993, 38.

WEB SITES

http://www.uky.edu/KGS/coal/webfossl/pages/arthros.htm
Information on fossilized insects plus good links to other sites

http://yucky.kids.discovery.com/flash/roaches/index.html
Information on cockroaches

http://24.114.7.13/kevin/Trilobites.html
Great site for trilobites!

http://www.science.uwaterloo.ca/earth/geoscience/millr7.html
Picture of giant millipede and its tracks

http://cricket.biol.sc.edu/usc-roach-cam.html
See live hissing cockroaches on this webcam!

Search strategies:

Use a search engine to search for insects by their names, or their names and the word *prehistoric* or *fossils*

Some examples:

Prehistoric dragonflies
Trilobites
Millipede fossils
Megarachne
Insect flight

GLOSSARY

abdomen (AB-doe-min)—The third part of an insect's body, behind the head and thorax.

amphibian (am-FIB-ee-an)—An animal that lives in water when it's young, breathing through gills, and then lives on land as an adult, breathing through lungs. Frogs, toads, newts, and salamanders are amphibians.

antenna, antennae (an-TEN-uh, an-TEN-ee)—One of two jointed feelers on an insect's head that it uses for sensing things.

arachnid (a-RACK-nid)—The group of arthropods that includes spiders, ticks, and mites. Arachnids have eight legs, and they do not have wings or antennae.

arthropod (AR-thruh-pod)—An animal with jointed legs and a hard outer skeleton. Crustaceans, centipedes, millipedes, insects, spiders, trilobites, scorpions, and eurypterids are arthropods.

caddis fly (CAD-is fly)—An insect with four wings that is related to moths and butterflies.

camouflage (CAM-uh-flahj)—The ability to blend in with one's surroundings.

cephalothorax (sef-uh-low-THOR-acks)—The joined head and thorax on spiders and arachnids.

chelicera, chelicerae (kee-LIS-er-uh, kee-LIS-er-ee)—The first pair of appendages near a spider's mouth which are used to grab prey.

compound eye—One large eye made up of many smaller lenses.

continent (CON-tin-ent)—A large mass of land that is separated from other land masses by oceans.

crustacean (cruh-STAY-shun)—One of the group of arthropods that includes crabs, lobsters, shrimp, and crayfish. Most of them live in the water.

evolve (ee-VOLV)—The process by which plants and animals gradually change with each new generation to adapt to their environment.

exoskeleton (ek-so-SKEL-uh-ton)—A hard shell-like outer skeleton that protects and supports the body.

facial suture (FAY-shul SOO-cher)—A seam in the shell of a trilobite.

genal spines (GEE-nul spinz)—Long spikes on both sides of a trilobite's body.

gills—A body organ that allows animals to breathe in water.

Gondwanaland (gond-WAH-nuh-land)—When Pangaea split into two continents two hundred million years ago, Gondwanaland was the southern continent that later became Africa, South America, Australia, and Antarctica.

head—The first part of an insect's body, to which its eyes, mouthparts, and antennae are attached.

horsetails—A plant with no flowers that is mainly a hollow jointed stem.

Hymenaea (hi-men-EE-uh)—A group of plants related to peas and beans whose sap became amber.

labial mask (LAY-bee-ul mask)—On a dragonfly nymph, an armlike lip which can grasp prey.

Laurasia (lo-RAY-shuh)—The northern continent, made up of North America and Asia, that split off from Pangaea two hundred million years ago.

maxilla, maxillae (mak-SILL-a, mak-SILL-ee)—Mouthparts of an insect.

metamorphosis (met-uh-MOR-fuh-sis)—A major change in the body structure and life habits of an insect; for instance, when a caterpillar changes into a butterfly.

molt—To shed an outer layer like an exoskeleton, so a new one can grow.

mygalomorphs (MIG-a-lo-morfs)—The group of spiders, also called "bird-eating spiders," that includes the tarantula.

node—A bump. Ants have a node on their waists, which distinguishes them from wasps.

ovipositor (OH-vee-poz-ih-tur)—A tube-shaped body part which female insects use to lay eggs.

Pangaea (pan-GEE-uh)—An ancient continent, from 220 million years ago, that was made up of all the modern continents joined together.

pedipalpi (ped-ih-PAL-pee)—On spiders and arachnids, the second pair of appendages near the mouth.

predator (PRED-uh-tor)—An animal that attacks and kills other animals, usually for food.

prey (pray)—An animal eaten by another animal for food.

pterosaur (TER-uh-sor)—An extinct flying reptile from the Jurassic and Cretaceous periods.

simple eye—An eye with only one lens.

spinneret (SPIN-ner-et)—The organ on a spider and some caterpillar's rear ends that secretes silk to make webs and cocoons.

telson (TEL-son)—The tail of a eurypterid or scorpion that might be used as a paddle, or that might include a stinger.

thorax (THOR-aks)—The middle section of an insect's body, to which its legs and wings are attatched.